Dinosauria and Prehistoric Creatures Magazine

Interview
With
Audrey Atuchin

Bring the past to life
With 3d printing

Learning about
Daspletosaurus
With Denver Fowler
And Elias Warshaw

Unpacking the
Fossil's crate
Brian Curtice PhD

Ankylosaurus
Discussed
With
Kenneth Carpenter

Chatting with
The
I know Dinos
Podcast

DINOSAURIA AND PREHISTORIC CREATURES MAGAZINE

Spring 2023

CONTENTS

65 MEETING THE MEN WHO REINTRODUCED DASPLETOSAURUS TO THE WORLD

46 DISCUSSING ANKYLOSAURUS WITH DR. KENNETH CARPENTER

By Shetan Noir

CHARLESTON FOSSIL TOURS

76

DINOSAURIAMAGAZINE@YAHOO.COM

HTTPS://SHETANNOIR.WIXSITE.COM/SQUATCHGQMAGAZINE

PALEO
NERDS

**Bringing the past to life with
3d printing.**

By Shetan Noir

Technology advances every year and brings with it a brighter future but when that same
Technology shines on the past, It is amazing what details emerge out of the shadows.
3d resin printing in proving to be a very powerful tool to aid paleontologist in bringing
ancient creatures back in full detail.
I chat with Denver Fowler on the Dickinson museum to learn more about the process.

**I very much enjoyed the fossil report. I am facinated with how much you can do
with a 3d printer. It is outstanding!**

(Denver Fowler)
The 3D printer lets us do a lot. The price of 3D printing and scanning has come right
down in the past 2-3 years. I never liked 3D printing until recently - printed fossils had
coarse print lines on them, and the printing process would often fail. This is because
people were using filament printers. In ~2020/2021, a local man brought some resin 3D
printed pieces into the museum to show me, and I was blown away by the quality. Resin
3D prints are much better than filament... and the prints we make are 0.05mm per layer,
whereas we can go down to 0.02mm per layer if we like, so better than double the
resolution!

The newest printers have such good resolution the constraint on detail in models is now
in the 3D model that you print from. 3D scanners have come down in price such that
you can get 0.2mm scan resolution in a $500 scanner, whereas you used to have to pay
$10000 but 0.2mm in a model does not compare to (effectively) 0.05 or 0.02mm
resolution of the printers. 0.2mm is the top level too, and most 3D scans do not get that
good. This means that 3D scans of big bones are ok, but if you want a little skull, or if
you want fine details like surfac epores etc, you need to use traditional rubber molding
and casting. Micro CT does ok, but you can only scan small objects.
However, I think visitors don't want to see a museum full of casts, and 3D prints are
effectively that, so you have to be careful.
Also, many of the 3D printed skulls and skeletons are sculpted 3D models, rather than
being scans of real fossils. Now, we do need to fill in missing pieces of skeletons or
skulls, and often fossils are flattened or distorted, such that we need to restore them to
some kind of 3D shape for exhibit.
I therefore take a particular approach when considering what we put on exhibit.

We printed a sculpture of a Pteranodon skeleton, so that we can hang a flying Pteranodon over the exhibit hall. I think that this is acceptable because almost all 3D flying pterosaurs that you see in museums are bascially sculptures. There are a few based on casts of real bones (Questzalcoatlus wing, probably a few Santana Fm skulls), but all the Pteranodons you see are sculpted, b/c the fossils are squashed flat.

full size Pteranodon for the exhibit
(yes, I put the fingers in the wrong
place for this photo)

In the coming year, we're going to mount a skeleton of the baby T.rex "Chomper" - once I get the description finished and out. Now, this is a fragmentary skull, so any mount is ~90% sculpted reconstruction. However, this is the only way you;re going to be able to see such a thing, so I think in this case also it is acceptable to have a 3D printed sculpture.
Right now, we're 3D scanning a new anylosaur species. We want to mount a skeleton, but the bones are fragile, so I'm going to mostly 3D print them. I will probably try to retrodeform some or all of the bones.
And, going back to the new species, Daspletosaurus wilsoni. We have about 30% of the skull, but we're lucky that it is mostly unrepeated bones. As such, we are scanning the bones we do have, then we will mirror and print them to complete the 2 sides of the skull. We then just need to add some midline bones (nasal, frontal, parietal, braincase) and we can have a complete skull on display.
I am deciding now how we will fill in those missing bones. If we got casts from another museum, then we'd have to negotiate a deal if we wanted to sell mini 3D prints of the complete D. wilsoni skull.
If I just get those parts sculted, they are less authentic in a way, but there are no permissions issues (I hesitate to say copyright, since you cannot own copyright on a natural structure - and you can't copyright federally owned fossils

The 3D printers could print out something probably 10 times as detailed as those.
Which means I could print out a 4cm long head and it would have all the detail of a 40cm head. Probably.

I saw the Daspletosaurus 3d printed head that was in the video. It looked very detailed

The Daspletosaurus print is nice-looking. The actual model it is printed from is medium or relatively low detail level. it wasnt ever intended to be used for 3D printing - Andrey just made it as an art guide (but he is so ridiculously talented that even his 3D "doodles" are breathtaking).

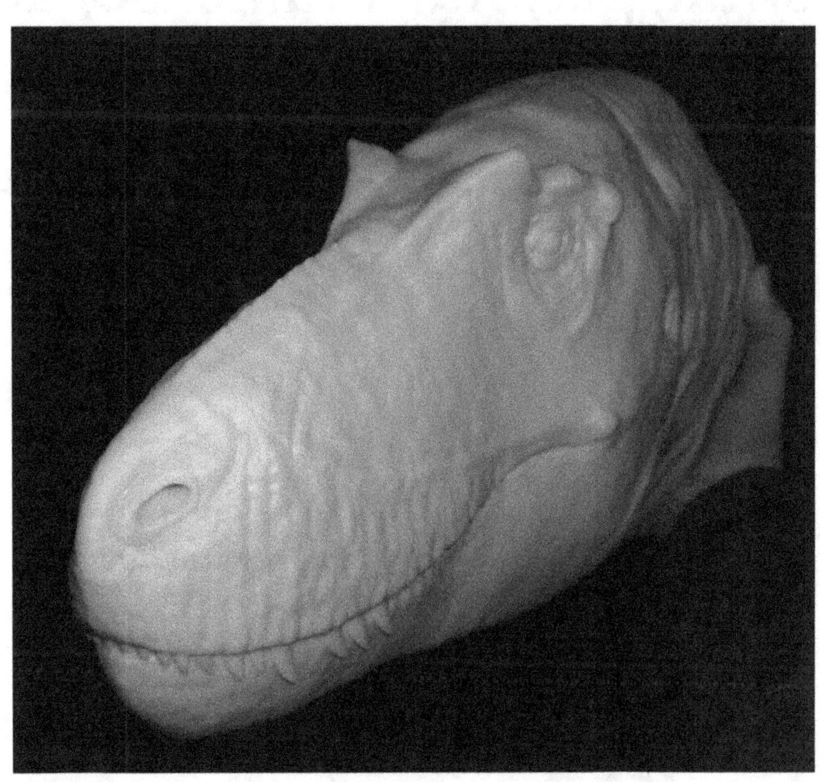

And, going back to the new species, Daspletosaurus wilsoni. We have about 30% of the skull, but we're lucky that it is mostly unrepeated bones. As such, we are scanning the bones we do have, then we will mirror and print them to complete the 2 sides of the skull. We then just need to add some midline bones (nasal, frontal, parietal, braincase) and we can have a complete skull on display.

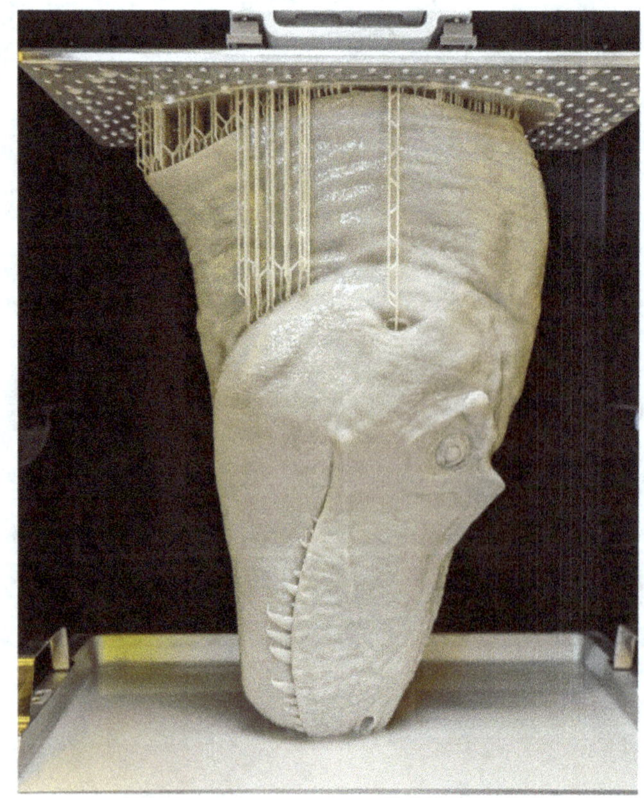

this is the skull printed, but somewhere I have a photo of it on the print plate

That is incredible, is that life sized?

it is the juvie from dino dantl monument (now in the Carnegie) so yes life sized

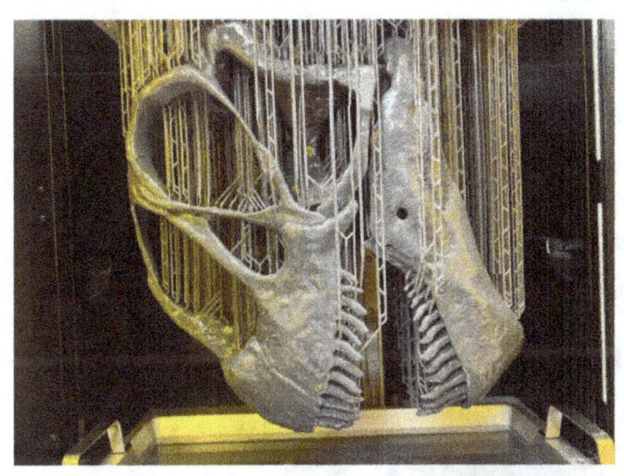

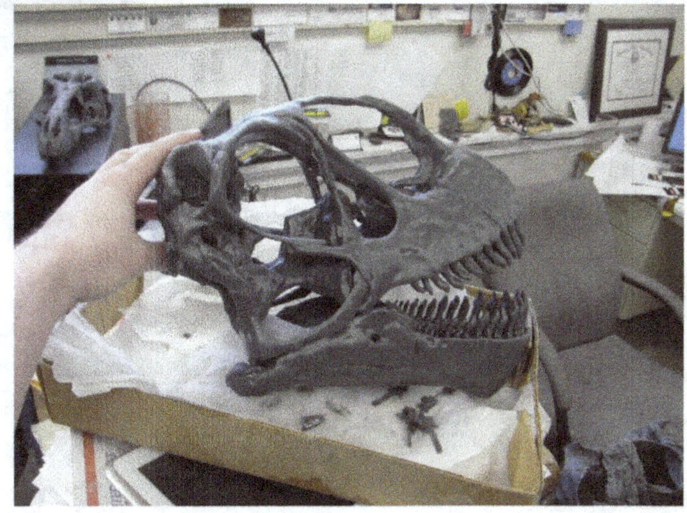

The newest printers have such good resolution the constraint on detail in models is now in the 3D model that you print from. 3D scanners have come down in price such that you can get 0.2mm scan resolution in a $500 scanner, whereas you used to have to pay $10000 but 0.2mm in a model does not compare to (effectively) 0.05 or 0.02mm resolution of the printers. 0.2mm is the top level too, and most 3D scans do not get that good. This means that 3D scans of big bones are ok, but if you want a little skull, or if you want fine details like surfac epores etc, you need to use traditional rubber molding and casting. Micro CT does ok, but you can only scan small objects.

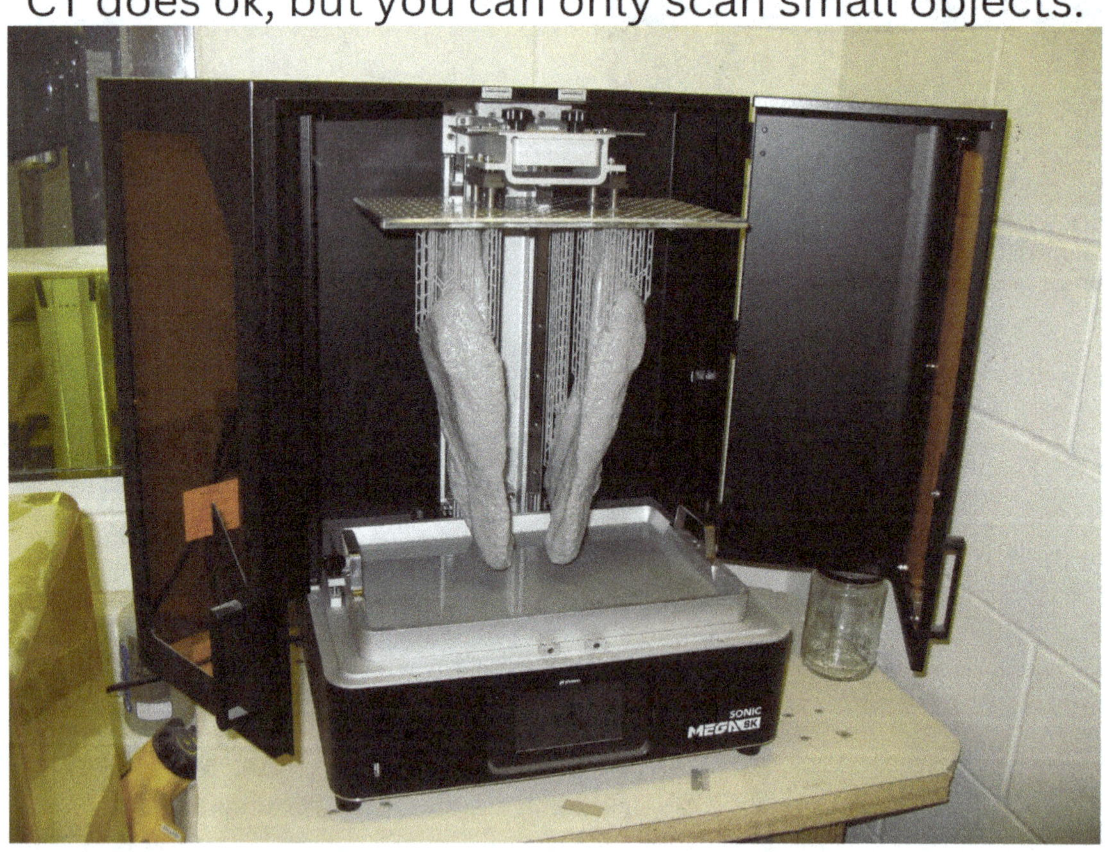

Will any of these 3d printed model be available to buy?

We've got some 3D prints of the Andrey Atuchin 3D model of Daspletosaurus wilsoni that are up for sale - this web page is not official yet as I am dealing with initial orders http://dickins

Ok, now I need to do a full article on 3d printing and it's value to paleontology exhibits

3D printing is interesting... I don't think anyone wants to go to a musuem that is only 3D prints

True but seeing exhibits with full skeletons or life like dinosaurs hold the wonder of these creatures.

I think 3D printing is good for filling in missing pieces, or showing skeletons for animals where they are usually crushed (e.g. pterosaurs) or making casts of very rare things like dino skulls.

and this one is on the daspletosaurus print page

What do you paint them with?

A normal undercoat, then regular acrylics, I don't sand them or anything.
well, my staff does not sand them! I am not especially good at painting casts.
My wife (Dr. Liz freedman Fowler) is the best!
most of these painted casts were painted by our 2022 intern Joel Crothers, or my Collections manager Amanda Hendrix

Right now, we're 3D scanning a new anylosaur species. We want to mount a skeleton, but the bones are fragile, so I'm going to mostly 3D print them. I will probably try to retrodeform some or all of the bones.

Tiktaalik skull being printed

Painted or not, I think they all look amazing.

The price of 3D printing is very cheap now, messy mind you but I think it is tricky for beginners as there are lots of things that can go wrong, but once you know what you are doing it goes ok .

That's true of most creative technology. I remember my first try at using my silhouette vinyl cutter.

We have one of those but I have never learned how to use it. I watched some videos but have not needed it yet
looks good for lettering and flat color symbols.

It's great for making stencils

basically when I started at my museum the only other staff member retired quickly, and so noone knew how to use the specialist equipment
yeah I need to learn how to use it really, There are good videos on youtube.

Thank you for discussing the 3d printing process.

miniature Crystal Palace
Iguanodon, about 10"

3D printed the missing part of a Triceratops frill

OWN A 3D PRINTED BUST OF THE NEW TYRANNOSAURID, DASPLETOSAURUS WILSONI

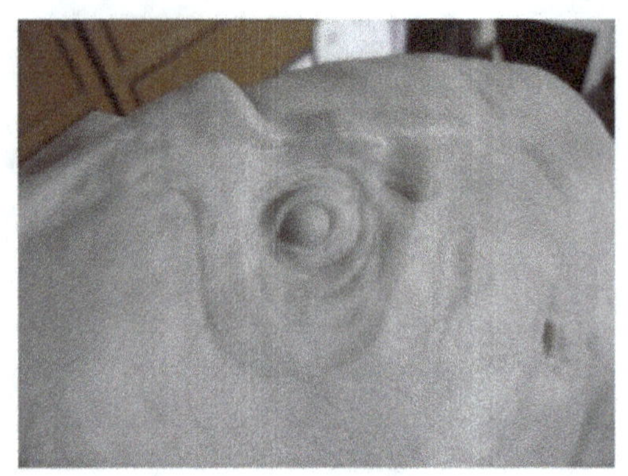

Macro closeup of eye detail on LARGE 40cm bust. No flash.

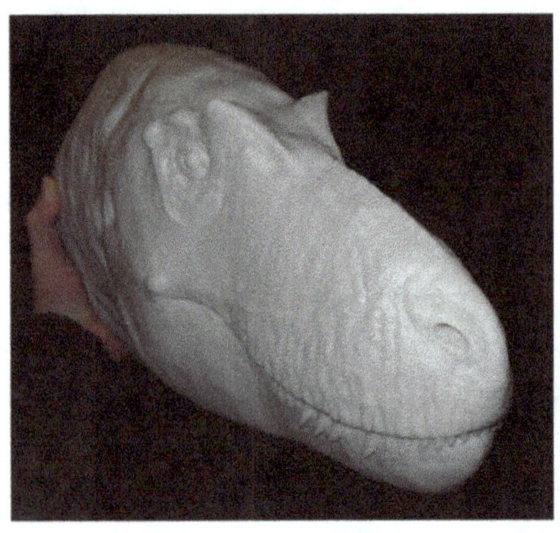

LARGE 40cm bust in pale grey. Flash.

<u>LARGE PRINTS</u>

- 40cm long
- **US$150** (plus shipping)

<u>MEDIUM PRINTS</u>

- 22cm long
- **US$50** (plus shipping)

We have arranged with Andrey to make 3D prints of this available for purchase. Andrey receives 12.5% of the gross, with remaining profits going into a fund for paleontology research at Badlands Dinosaur Museum. Each of the large prints takes 48hrs to print out, so these are therefore in limited supply (we need our printer for exhibit and research projects!).

http://dickinsonmuseumcenter.com/badlands_research-2022newtyranno-busts/

Mounted skeleton (NCSM 14345) at the North Carolina Museum of Natural Sciences.

high-spined lizard') is a genus of carcharodontosaurid dinosaur that existed in what is now North America during the Aptian and early Albian stages of the Early Cretaceous, from 113 to 110 million years ago. Like most dinosaur genera, Acrocanthosaurus contains only a single species, A. atokensis.

Acrocanthosaurus was among the largest theropods known to exist, with an estimated skull length of 1.23 m (4.0 ft) and body length of 11–11.5 m (36–38 ft) based on the largest known specimen. Researchers have yielded body mass estimates for this specimen between 4.4 and 6.6 metric tons (4.9 and 7.3 short tons) based on various techniques.

Exploring Paleoart
with Mr. Audrey Atuchin

By Shetan Noir

Can you please tell us more about your background?

I was born in Russia and graduated from the university as a biologist. I was engaged in scientific research in the field of entomology. Although all my life I was fond of paleontology, dinosaurs and other extinct animals, collecting fossils, but I did not have the opportunity to do this professionally or study paleontology at the university.

How did you become interested in paleoart?

I have always been very interested in illustrations in books, which were quite rare when I was a teenager and I really missed it. Then, at one point, I wanted to try to visualize the dinosaurs the way I wanted to, the way I saw them, reconstruct based on the skeleton, try to see these animals again, as if they were alive now and looked realistic. Probably I wanted to resurrect them, and I also like to draw.

Your paleoart is wonderful, I saw your depiction of Daspletosaurus wilsoni in a recent paper and it looks amazingly! How do you create your artwork?

Thank you! As a rule, I begin my work on the reconstruction of some organism by carefully studying what we know about it, the fossil itself as well as studying all the scientific papers that are related to it. Also, the paleontologists with whom I work and for whom I create these illustrations play a huge role, we discuss, consult, etc. Then I often create a sculpture to see it all in 3D, to understand how it works and how it looks, to reconstruct it based on bones. This reconstruction then helps me create a 2D illustrations, draw it how I want, include it in the environment or without it. Now I mainly paint with digital brushes in Photoshop, but there was a time when I painted with watercolors, ink and used other art media including polymer clay.

I also saw artwork of one of my favorite prehistoric creatures the Scutosaurus on your page. What is your favorite dinosaurs to illustrate?

This is a very common question that I get asked. I don't have a favorite dinosaur or other animal actually, I love everything I do. Let's just say my current favorite is usually the one I'm working on at the moment. I study it, try to imagine it alive and love it.

What other books or projects has your artwork appeared in?

I have participated in the publishing of many books on paleontology and dinosaurs, both in Russian and in other languages. Although, most of all I am involved in working on museum expositions and on illustrations for press releases and scientific papers. You can find my illustrations and murals in museums around the world, most of all in the USA, Canada and Australia, especially in the Smithsonian National Museum of Natural History, the Denver Museum of Nature and Science, the Natural History Museum of Utah and, the Queensland Museum.

Will we be seeing more paleoart from you in the future?

Well, since this is my full-time work and the source of earnings, then of course you will see a lot of my artworks in the future. I hope that I will be ok. Although, the specifics of my work is that many of my commissions are often embargoed for a long time and I cannot publish them, so for a long time you may not see any news from me, but this does not mean that I have stopped. I work every day and almost without days off.

Can people order prints of your artwork?

Yes, there are some shops that sell prints of my artworks. But that's not much. I've been wanting to get into selling prints for a long time, but I'm putting it off because I'm too busy.

What else would you like to tell us about your paleoart?

Well, I don't know. It is important for me to be immersed in the work, not just to be an artist. I participate in dinosaur excavations, study fossils, do preparation work with fossils. Although, I don't consider myself an artist in the broadest sense, I prefer to research, study and make discoveries.

Where can people go to see your artwork and keep up to date with your new illustrations?

The easiest way is to just google my name. I am in many social networks, where I try to share my new artworks, news and publications whenever possible. The main ones are instagram, twitter, facebook. I also have a gallery on Devianart, but I rarely go there and update it.

https://www.palaeocast.com/

https://terribleliz ards.libsyn.com/ website

Getting to know the I KNOW DINO Podcast

By Shetan Noir

Thanks for the questions! Let us know when the issue comes out.

Can you please tell us more about your backgrounds?

Sure! We're Garret and Sabrina, a husband and wife team who produce the weekly dinosaur podcast I Know Dino. We started podcasting eight years ago because we wanted to stay up to date on all the latest dinosaur discoveries (there's a new one every week)!

Our backgrounds are not exactly dinosaur-related. Garret's background is in engineering and Sabrina worked for years in various industries, including journalism, book publishing, education, and tech. When we decided to launch the podcast we had a lot of learning to do, but fortunately our backgrounds helped us understand the technical terms and produce the show.

How did you become interested in the Dinosaurs?

We both loved dinosaurs as kids. Sabrina nearly wore out her VHS tape of *Land Before Time*, and Garret did wear out his favorite *Stegosaurus* hat.

We both had lots of dinosaur books and stuffed animals, and loved looking at pictures of these awesome animals.

Like many kids, our interests changed as teenagers. But we rediscovered our love of dinosaurs together when we lived near the American Museum of Natural History and we were able to visit often.

Can you tell us more about your podcast, I Know Dino?

I Know Dino is a weekly show where we cover the latest dinosaur news, talk to dinosaur experts, and dive deep on specific dinosaurs.

In addition to the podcast, we have books, merchandise such as t-shirts, and a website full of resources, including a virtual map of dinosaur museums around the world and dinosaur-themed lesson plans for elementary, middle, and high school students.

How did you start your podcast?

We had a dinosaur-themed wedding, and after the wedding, we didn't want to stop talking about dinosaurs.

We noticed at the time that while there were, and still are, some great paleontology podcasts, there weren't any weekly podcasts dedicated to dinosaurs.

So we decided to start our podcast. Garret had been listening to podcasts for a while at that point, which gave us an idea of what format and segments we wanted in our show. We reached out to paleontologists to interview them for our show and did lots of research.

There was a learning curve, and we made some mistakes in the beginning, but we heard from some listeners that it was fun for them to be on the learning journey with us.

Where can people listen to your podcast?

On your favorite podcast platform! I Know Dino is available for free on all the major podcast apps, including:

- Apple Podcasts
- Spotify
- Google Podcasts
- Amazon Music

Just search for "dinosaur podcast" or "i know dino."

You can also listen to episodes on our website at iknowdino.com.

What topics are you most interested in talking about on your show?

Pretty much anything dinosaur-related, we're open to talking about. A big part of our show is talking through the latest dinosaur discoveries, and our "dinosaur of the day" segment, where we dive deep into a dinosaur one of our listeners requested.

We also love talking to dinosaur experts, whether they be paleontologists, paleoartists, writers, game developers, or some other type of expert. We've even interviewed a dinosaur dancer!

Recently we launched our semi-regular "dinosaur connection challenge" segment, where our community gives us a random topic and we tie it back to dinosaurs. Past challenges include sandwiches, chocolate, and the *Titanic*.

What is your most popular episode?

Our first episode is our most downloaded episode, but it's closely followed by our 300thepisode, "Spinosaurus revisited" (iknowdino.com/Spinosaurus-Episode-300/). We interviewed paleontologist and spinosaur expert Nizar Ibrahim, and we discussed in depth everything we knew about the enigmatic*Spinosaurus*so far, including how the holotype fossils were destroyed in WWII, and how Ibrahim tracked down the neotype in Morocco.

What are your favorite Dinosaurs or Prehistoric creatures?

Sabrina's favorite dinosaur is*Brontosaurus*and Garret's is*Ankylosaurus*. We also both really like therizinosaurs, because they're so weirdly cool.

Is there anything else you want to tell us?

Our I Know Dino community iswhat makes our podcast so special. We're "di-know-it-alls" who all love dinosaurs and science.

One of the best parts of producing I Know Dino is connecting with our community and getting to know amazing people from around the world. We do this mainly through our Patreon (patreon.com/iknowdino).

People who join can take part in our Discord server and chat with everyone about dinosaurs all day, every day. They can also request a "dinosaur of the day", get shoutouts, and easily give us feedback on the show.

Do you have any social media sites or a website?

You can find us on our website,iknowdino.comand on YouTube atyoutube.com/c/iknowdino.

We're also on social media:

- Instagram:@iknowdino
- Facebook:iknowdino
- Twitter:@iknowdino
- TikTok:@iknowdino

And if you want to join our community of di-know-it-alls, check outpatreon.com/iknowdino.

I KNOW
DINO
The Big Dinosaur Podcast
Support us on www.patreon.com/iknowdino

I KNOW
DINO
THE BIG
DINOSAUR
PODCAST

PALAEO
AFTER DARK

The Dinosaur Farm

https://www.dinosaurfarm.com/

Toys * Books* and all things dinosaur

Sinankylosaurus zhuchengensis

"Zhucheng's Chinese Fused Lizard"

A new member of the Ankylosauria from China, Sinankylosaurus zhuchengensis, was named in July 2020. It means "Zhucheng's Chinese Fused Lizard" and was excavated in the Zhucheng area, northeast China, in rocks approximately 75 million years old. It was named by Wang et al. 2020 based off of a single hip bone, the right ilium. Ankylosaurids are walking tanks: heavily armored, low to the ground, and adorned with spikes, scutes, and tail clubs. They would have been a difficult meal for any predator unless they could flip them onto their soft underbelly.

The Zhucheng locale in the northeast of China has produced tyrannosaurs (Zhuchengtyrannus, a close relative of Tyrannosaurus

www. Fossilcrates.com

hadrosaurs (Shantungosaurus, compares favorably to Edmontosaurus, both regions have produced numerous named hadrosaurs), ceratopsians (Sinoceratops, Udanoceratops, Ischioceratops, and Zhuchengceratops in China and over a dozen named ceratopsians from the United States), sauropods (Zhuchengtitan from China, though no northern North America sauropods are yet known, Alamosaurus was present in North America), pachycephalosaurs (Micropachycephalosaurus from China, Pachycephalosaurus from North America), oviraptorosaurs (Anomalipes from China, Caenagnathus and Anzu from North America), ornithopods, small theropods, and now... more ankylosaurs!

This find continues to demonstrate the startling similarity between the Late Cretaceous faunas of North America's Campanian and Maastrichtian rocks compared to those of China's Wangshi Group.
Sinankylosaurus was found in the Wang's Group of the Upper Cretaceous in Zhucheng City, Shandong Province, and is 73.5 - 77.3 Ma (Campanian age).
The holotype, or name-bearing bone used to compare Sinankylosaurus to all other dinosaurs, is ZJZ-183, a right ilium housed at the Zhucheng Dinosaur Culture Research Center (image below)

Figure 1. Image of ZJZ-183, right ilium holotype of Sinankylosaurus, ~65cm long, 40 cm wide. (a) is the ventral view, (b) is the "back" view

What follows is my interpretation of a Google translation of their paper (all translation errors are mine). It gets heavy in the details but I hope you find it interesting to see how paleontologists go about making comparisons to other animals when they are trying to determine if their discovery is new or can be assigned to an existing animal.

Wang et al. 2020 list the following characters as a combination unique to Sinankylosaurus:

The back of the ilium is smooth
The acetabular protrusion is developed
A wide "wing", anterior twist, acetabular protrusion posterior (distal)
The process of extending to the proximal end strongly shrinks and narrows
The rear end has a large gap in width

BC's Figure 2. Comparative ilia images from Wang et al. 2020.

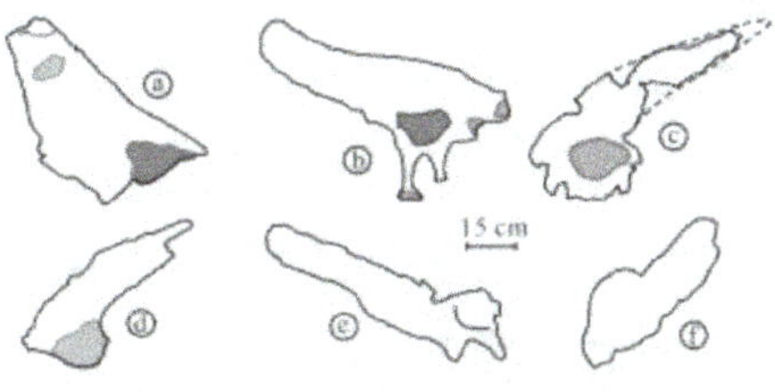

图 3　诸城中国甲龙(a)、金城洮河龙(b)、丽水浙江龙(c)、谷氏绘龙相似种(d)、中国缙云甲龙(e)和步氏克氏龙(f)肠骨腹视对比

Fig. 3　Ilium in ventral view of *Sinankylosaurus zhuchengensis* (a) compared with that of *Taohelong jinchengensis*(b), *Zhejiangosaurus lishuiensis*(c), *Pinacosaurus* cf. *grangeri*(d), *Jinyunpelta sinensis*(e) and *Crichtonsaurus bohlini*(f)

The authors compare ZJZ-183 to a number of Ankylosauria (the group ankylosaurids, nodosaurids, and polacanthids belong to). I address each of their comparisons in the order they do in the paper.

Comparison to other Chinese Ankylosauria

Pinacosaurus cf. grangeri

R 264 is the specimen number assigned to "A nearly complete sacrum and the articulated right ilium..." that was collected by T'an at Tianqiaotun in April of 1923, making it the earliest recorded ankylosaur fossil collected in China. Buffetaut called it Pinacosaurus cf. grangeri. Wang et al. 2020 state, "R264 has broad 'wings', that is, very broad ilium bones. In appearance, shape, curvature, and appearance and direction of ridges on the mid-abdominal surface."

Their comparison to a specimen they labeled Zpal MgD-II/1, a left ilium, calling it "Gu's painted dragon in Warsaw" and stating it is "very similar to Buffetaut (1995)", meaning Pinacosaurus cf. grangeri. I interpreted this section as Wang et al. 2020 are agreeing with the synonymy of P. ningshiensis with P. grangeri, and thus ZPAL MgD-II/1 and R 264 belong to the same type of animal. The presence of ridges on these specimens means they are not the same animal as ZJZ-183.

Jinyunpelta Sinensis

Jinyunpelta is the most primitive and oldest known true ankylosaurid and possesses a cool tail club. Wang et al. 2020 compared ZJZ-183 with Jinyunpelta. Jinyunpelta's left ilium "is wider, and the contraction of the front protrusion is weaker than Sinankylosaurus", the "...acetabular protrusion is relatively degree weaker than that of Sinankylosaurus", and "...the acetabulum width of the protrusion from the distal end to the proximal end varies more". Thus they conclude ZJZ-183 cannot be referred to Jinyunpelta which I agree with.

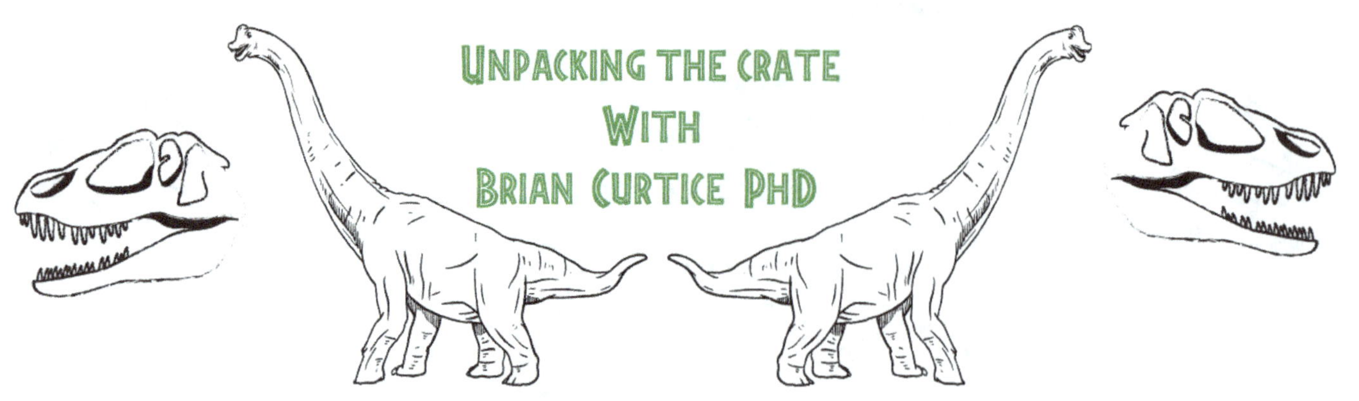

Crichtonsaurus bohlini

Crichtonsaurus is a Late Cretaceous ankylosaurid that may not be a valid taxon because of some issues with the material referred to it by previous paleontologists. However, a nearly complete left ilium (LPM 101-3) has been referred to Crichtonsaurus and, though it may belong to a different genus than Crichtonsaurus, Wang et al. 2020 rightly compared ZJZ-183 to LPM 101-3 and observed ZJZ-183 "is significantly wider than LPM 101-3, and the width shrinks when extending forward. The degree is also significantly stronger." Additionally, the "Wide distal end, raised back, narrowed forward..." make it at once different from ZJZ-183. Whatever LPM 101-3 ultimately comes to be called it clearly belongs to a different genus than ZJZ-183.

Zhejiangosaurus lishuiensis

Zhejiangosaurus is a Late Cretaceous nodosaurid with both left and right ilia preserved, their "...acetabular protruding middle back. The surface is convex, there are obvious ridges, and a deep longitudinal direction is formed on the ventral surface.". Wang et al. 2020 note, "The extension direction of the dorsal ridge of the acetabular protrusion is different from that of Zhejiangosaurus. Similarly, there is no longitudinal depression on the ventral surface, and the acetabular anterior of Zhejiangosaurus, the protrusion is significantly narrower and slender than the acetabular protrusion in ZJZ-183." Their conclusion means ZJZ-183 does not belong to Zhejiangosaurus, which I agree with. However, it doesn't automatically mean ZJZ-183 is not a nodosaurid.

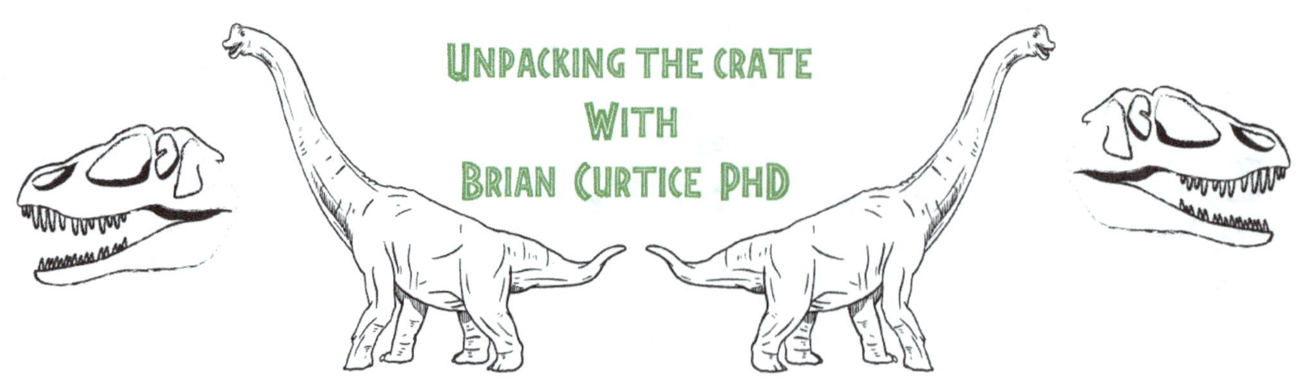

Taohelong jinchengensis

Taohelong is the first polacanthid discovered in China. Wang et al. 2020 compared ZJZ-183 to Taohelong and write, "Most of the surface [of Taohelong] is a long oval shallow depression, and its outer edge is backward. The ridges continue to the top of the acetabular fossa." They further compare ZJZ-183, noting a "Protrusion of the acetabulum There is a nearly circular depression on the ventral surface, which does not continue to the acetabular fossa. The square ridge, the acetabular protrusion of both contracted forward and narrowed, the latter. The degree of forward extension and contraction is more intense, and the former [Taohelong] has two acetabular protrusions. The width of the end has relatively little change.", concluding ZJZ-183 does not belong to Taohelong but does have some polacanthid similarity. Polacanthids are "halfway" between nodosaurids and ankylosaurids so it isn't surprising to me there is some resemblance in the bones with these specimens.

Wang et al. 2020 Conclusion

Their initial analysis wasn't able to determine if Sinankylosaurus belongs to the Ankylosauridae, Nodosauridae, or Polacanthidae. Ankylosaurs have wide skulls, short acetabular processes, and large tail clubs, nodosaurs have pear-shaped skulls, long acetabular processes, and no tail clubs, while polacanthids have a blend of characters between them.

The ZJZ-183 acetabular process "is distorted, but it is relative to the acetabular protrusion of the ankylosaurids", however, "The degree of forward contraction of the acetabular protrusion is more intense, which is similar to that of the polacanthids." My instincts say it belongs to the Ankylosauridae and would have had an awesome tail club, which is how I asked our artist to illustrate it for this blog. I will leave the final word with Google translate, which produced this as the final sentence in the paper regarding the family affinity of Sinankylosaurus, "It seems, therefore, Sinankylosaurus belongs to Ankylosauridae and Nodosauridae or Polacanthidae, family is still uncertain. It is determined that its ownership needs to be further confirmed by new fossil materials." The story of all paleontologists the world over and the reason we keep seeking fossils, to solve these relationship riddles!

https://www.fossilcrates.com/blogs/news/sinankylo
saurus-zhuchengensis-the-new-addition-to-the-
armored-dinosaur-family

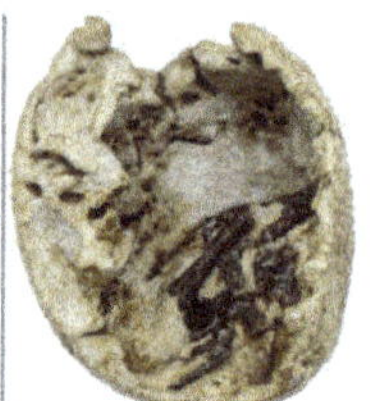

https://www.fossilcrates.com/

Make sure to also check out

https://www.paleoportals.com

THE ETCHES COLLECTION

MUSEUM OF JURASSIC
MARINE LIFE

Discussing Ankylosuarus with Dr. Kenneth Carpenter

By Shetan Noir

Can you please tell us more about your background?

I decided to become a paleontologist at an early age. My mother took me to see the *Godzilla* (the original) when I was five. This decision was reinforced when I found a partial ground sloth skeleton when I was 15. I helped the Denver Museum of Natural History excavate it. The following year I found the forelimb of a *Stegosaurus* in the vicinity of the Marsh and Cope dinosaur sites in Canon City. In college, I struggled as a student and dropped out for about five years. Then went back and struggled some more, but during this period I did a one semester apprenticeship in the fossil lab at the Smithsonian. By the time I got my undergraduate degree I had already published several scientific papers in paleontology. I went on to work in various museums mounting fossil skeletons for display and eventually ended up at the Denver Museum, where I stayed for about 22 years. Then I went to be director at the Prehistoric Museum in Price, Utah.

You are the retired director of USU Eastern prehistoric museum, Can you tell us about that museum?

The Prehistoric Museum was a joint project begun in 1961 between what was then Carbon College and Price City. It was operated mostly by volunteers until the 1990s. The founding director, Don Burge, did the best he could, although many of the exhibits and collections still looked amateurish when I arrived in 2010. The museum always seemed to me like it had great potential, but needed someone with decades of museum experience to raise it and the exhibits to professional museum standards. That is where I came in and what I basically did for the 10 years I was there. When I retired there was still much more to do, and hopefully the staff I hired can see it to completion.

I had to look this up since I never bothered to keep track. My name is associated with the following:

Ankylosaurs:

*Animantarx ramaljonesi*Carpenter, Kirkland, Burge, and Bird 1999

*Cedarpelta bilbeyhallorum*Carpenter, Kirkland, Burge, and Bird 2001

*Gargoyleosaurus parkpinorum*Carpenter, Miles and Cloward 1998

*Gastonia lorriemcwhinneyae*Kinneer, Carpenter, Shaw 2016

*Kunbarrasaurus ieversi*Leahey, Molnar, Carpenter, Witmer, and Salisbury 2015

*Mymoorapelta maysi*Kirkland and Carpenter 1994

*Niobrarasaurus coleii*Carpenter, Dilkes, and Weishampel 1995

*Peloroplites cedrimontanus*Carpenter, Bartlett, Bird, and Barrick 2009

Mammal:

*Docodon apoxys*Rougier, Sheth, Carpenter, Appella-Guiscafre, and Davis 2015

Ornithopods:

*Camptosaurus aphanoecetes*Carpenter and Wilson 2008

*Cedrorestes crichtoni*Gilpin, DiCroce and Carpenter 2006

*Dryosaurus elderae*Galton and Carpenter 2018

Planicoxa depressus(Gilmore 1909) Carpenter and Wilson 2008

*Planicoxa venenica*Dicroce and Carpenter 2001

*Proplanicoxa galtoni*Ishida and Carpenter 2010

*Sellacoxa pauli*Ishida and Carpenter 2010

*Theiophytalia kerri*Brill and Carpenter 2006

Plesiosaurs:

Libonectes morgani(Welles, 1949) Carpenter 1997

*Megacephalosaurus eulerti*Schumacher, Carpenter, and Everhart 2013

*Plesiopleurodon wellesi*Carpenter 1996

Pterosaur

*Harpactognathus gentryii*Carpenter, Unwin, Cloward, Miles, and Miles 2003

*Kepodactylus insperatus*Harris and Carpenter 1996

Sauropod:

*Cedarosaurus weiskopfae*Tidwell, Carpenter, and Brooks 1999

Maraapunisaurus fragillimus(Cope 1878) Carpenter 2018

Stegosaur

Alcovasaurus longispinus(Gilmore 1914) Galton and Carpenter 2016

*Hesperosaurus mjosi*Carpenter, Miles, Cloward 2001

Theropods

*Gojirasaurus quayi*Carpenter 1997

*Pectinodon bakkeri*Carpenter 1982

*Tanycolagreus topwilsoni*Carpenter, Miles, and Cloward

I am facinated by the armored Dinosaurs like the Ankylosaurias, Can we discuss that group of Dinosaurs?

We know they were Vegans based on their teeth, which look like your hand with the fingers together; these were not the serrated steak-knives of carnivorous dinosaurs. The skull bones tended to fuse together and become rough and pitted. They had squat, wide bodies and waddled on four short legs, yet managed to spread to all the continents. Their bodies were encased with bone disks and plates embedded in the skin, much like that seen on the backs of alligators and crocodiles. Like the Far Side cartoon (Gary Larson) said: Ankylosaurs are crunchy on the outside and soft and chewy on the inside. That about sums it up.

What drew your interest to the amoured Dinosaurs like Ankylosaurus and Stegasarus?

Back when I was an undergraduate, there was little interest in ankylosaurs and stegosaurs among paleontologists. The only two were Peter Galton on stegosaurs and Walter Coombs on ankylosaurs. Ankylosaurs were the ugly, unloved step-children among dinosaurs, so naturally I was attracted to them. Besides, most of them have ugly faces that only a mother (or paleontologist) could love

In my research I noticed that you had named Gargoyleosaurus Parkinorum, Can you tell us more about it?

When the bones and skull of *Gargoyleosaurus* were found in the mid-1990s, Jurassic ankylosaurs were little known and nothing of the skull. *Gargoyleosaurus* comes from near where the American Museum of Natural History dug at Bone Cabin Quarry in central Wyoming from 1898–1905. What is surprising is how advanced the skeleton was, having most all of the features that characterize the later Cretaceous ankylosaurs, including sculpted, fused skull bones and body encased in bone plates. The most primitive aspect of the skeleton is actually the open hip socket. In Cretaceous forms, the socket is a cup-shaped pocket into which the head of the thigh bone (femur) fits. *Gargoleosaurus* still retained the hip socket that you can see through, just like most dinosaurs. Fortunately, the people at Western Paleontology Labs, who found the original specimen, recognized the armor was partially arranged as in life and made a map, which allowed me to later make a fairly accurate reconstruction of the armor on the body. What we know about *Gargoyleosaurus* was made possible by Cliff Miles at Western Paleontology Labs and Bob Simons who donating the skeleton and pelvis.

Can you also tell us more about Gastonia Burgei?

The ankylosaur genus *Gastonia*, has two species:*Gastonia burgei* and *Gastonia lorriemcwhinneyae*. They are both from the Lower Cretaceous Cedar Mountain Formation, but *G. burgei*is geologically the older of the two being found at lower (=older) stratigraphic levels. Both species were found at sites with multiple specimens suggesting that *Gastonia*was a social animal. So, how shall we refer to them? A gaggle of *Gastonia*? Group? Pod? Gang? Pack? Herd? School? Army? Troop? Mob? Pride? Parliament?

Gastonia shares some unique features of the skull and skeleton that show a close evolutionary relationship with *Gargoyleosaurus* and *Mymoorapelta.*In fact, Jim Kirkland and I believe that these three can be grouped with *Polacanthus* into the family Polacanthidae. But not all paleontologists agree.

And Cedarpelta Bilbeyhallorum

This ankylosaur seems closely related to *Shamosaurus* and *Gobisaurus* from the Lower Cretaceous of Asia. All three share a boxy skull with a relatively long skull and probably lacked a tail club, and have been group into the Shamosaurine ankylosaurids (but not all paleontologists agree). The group probably originated in North America and migrated to Asia when a land bridge was established during the Early Cretaceous.*Cedarpelta*has peg-like teeth at the front of the mouth, rather than a beak, which is considered a primitive trait. The skull was found high in the Cedar Mountain Formation in deposits that have other dinosaurs more similar to those from Asia than Europe, hence the indication of a connection at this time with Asia as the North American plate separated from Europe.

How did you decide on Mymoorapelta Maysi as a name for an Ankylosaurus?

The names were created by coauthor Jim Kirkland. The genus (*Mymoorapelta*) honors Peter and Marilyn Mygatt and John D. and Vanetta Moore, who discovered the Mygatt-Moore Quarry, and *pelta*- Greek for shield. The species was named for Chris Mays, president of Dinamation International Corporation and founder of the Dinamation International Society, which funded the research into the specimens. In other words, Mays' shield from Mygatt-Moore. Dinosaurs are frequently named after people, although it is more common to restrict this to the species, like *Gastonia burgei*, which is named for Robert Gaston, who found the site producing the specimen, and Don Burge, who led the excavation.

Peloroplites Cedrimontanus is considered one of the bigger nodosaurids, but is there a bigger species out there?

There are definitely bones that indicate specimens as large or larger than *Peloroplites*, including a gigantic skull of *Ankylosaurus* indicating an individual almost 25 feet long. The reconstructed skeleton of *Gobisaurus*is certainly as big or maybe a little bigger than *Peloroplites.*

Did all Ankylosaurus have osteoderms for armor and clubbed tails?

The genus *Ankylosaurus* does have a body encased in armor and a big bone club, as does related ankylosaurs like *Euoplocephalus* and *Saichania*. These form the family Ankylosauridae. But other ankylosaurs did not have tail clubs, although they did have armor covered bodies. This includes *Edmontonia* and *Panoplosaurus* of the family Nodosauridae, and *Gastonia*,*Mymoorapelta* and *Gargoyleosaurus* of the family Polacanthidae

In a family tree with so many interesting species,Which ones stand out the most to you or are your favorites?

This question is related to the question I am often asked: What is your favorite dinosaur? The answer is what ever one I am currently writing about. In this case, it is *Camptosaurus* because that is the dinosaur I am currently writing about with Peter Galton.

What environments were the Ankylosaurus living in and what parts of the world have fossils been found?

Ankylosaurs have been found on every continent, including Antarctica long before it was encased in ice. They were a successful group appearing in Europe during the Early Jurassic, around 190 million years ago, and survived until the end of the Cretaceous around 66 million years ago. It is debatable whether they went extinct along with several other dinosaurs before the asteroid impact.

We know the environment ankylosaurs lived in from the rocks in which the fossils were found. *Pinacosaurus* specimens are from sand dune deposits, so it was clearly adapted to that harsh environment. In contrast *Ankylosaurus* and *Euoplocephalus* are from lowland river and floodplain deposits containing plant fossils suggesting a wet, coastal

environment like the Gulf Coast states of Louisiana and Mississippi. The oddest rocks with ankylosaurs is the Niobrara Formation, which was deposited in the Cretaceous sea that divided North America. All half-dozen or so specimens of the ankylosaur *Niobrarasaurus* are only known from those marine rocks. Does that mean *Niobrarasaurus* fed on algae like the marine iguana of the Galapagos, or is it more likely that these are of individuals that lived along the coast and whose dead bodies floated to sea?I suspect that latter, but like to imagine the possibility of the former.

Do paleontologist have any Insight into how intelligent the Ankylosauria group were, were some species more intelligent than others?

The brain size of ankylosaurs is known from casts made of the inside of the brain cavity and CT scans of the brain case. Compared to some other dinosaurs, the brain was not all that big, implying it was not the brightest animal on the planet. I picture it as like the Far Side cartoon of the *Stegosaurus* that managed to walk into the only tree around. But, if your mission in life is to eat and reproduce, then I guess ankylosaurs had just the right size brains. After all, they were extremely successful as a group, spreading to all the continents and surviving for at least 124 million years.

What were the major predators of the Ankylosaurus?

The genus *Ankylosaurus*is found in the same deposits as *Tyrannosaurus rex* .It is certainly possible that *T. rex* munched on young *Ankylosaurus*, but it might be harder to tackle an adult. *Euoplocephalus*is found in the same rocks as *Gorgosaurus* and *Daspletosaurus*. *Cedarpelta* and *Animantarx* are found in rocks that contained the large theropod *Siats*, while *Gargoyleosaurus* and *Mymoorapelta*co-occur with *Allosaurus* and *Torvosaurus*. Clearly, have a body encased in bone disks embedded in the skin was a great advantage for living in a world of big teeth.

Is there anything else you would like to tell us about Ankylosauria?

Just that they probably would not make good pets. They are not cuddly because they would probably break your couch if they climb up to join you. Not smart enough to fetch, can't roll over because then they would get stuck like a turtle, would poop all over your yard, and probably crash your backyard fence and get into your neighbor's garden.

Are there any books you would like our readers to know about?

For readers that want a book about dinosaurs that goes into more depth than the typical dinosaur book, then I suggest my book *"Acrocanthosaurus* Inside and Out"* published by Oklahoma University Press (available through Amazon or the publisher). It basically explains how paleontologists know what they know about dinosaurs, using *Acrocanthosaurus*as an example.

Where can people find out more about your research and work?

Most of my scientific papers and a few less technical articles can be downloaded free from Researchgate:
https://www.researchgate.net/profile/Kenneth_Carpenter3

ACROCANTHOSAURUS

INSIDE AND OUT

KENNETH CARPENTER

Fossil skeleton, Denver Museum of Nature and Science

GARGOYLEOSAURUS

Gargoyleosaurus (meaning "gargoyle lizard") is one of the earliest ankylosaurs known from reasonably complete fossil remains. The holotype was discovered in 1995 at the Bone Cabin Quarry West locality, in Albany County, Wyoming in exposures of the Upper Jurassic (Kimmeridgian to Tithonian stages) Morrison Formation

The type species, G. parkpinorum (originally G. parkpini) was described by Ken Carpenter et al. in 1998. A mounted skeletal reconstruction of Gargoyleosaurus parkpinorum can be seen at the Denver Museum of Nature and Science and, alongside a couple skeletons of baby Stegosaurus, has been on display there since around 2002. Gargoyleosaurus was present in stratigraphic zone 2 of the Morrison Formation.

Gargoyleosaurus was a relatively small ankylosaur, reaching 3–3.5 m (9.8–11.5 ft) in length and 300–754 kg (661–1,662 lb) in body mass

Welcome to The Museum getting to known Dr. Denver Fowler

By Shetan Noir

I'm originally from the UK. I did my undergraduate and master's degrees in England, then I went to the Museum of the Rockies to do a PhD under Dr. Jack Horner.

How did you become interested in paleontology?

I have a collecting background. When I was about 5 or 6 years old my family went on a holiday to Weymouth, on the Jurassic Coast of the southern United Kingdom. When playing on the beach, I found the impression of a fairly large (~6") ammonite in a boulder and dragged it back to my parents (which took me about 20 minutes). My dad had an interest in fossils, so he took us fossil hunting to the beach Charmouth, nearby. From that point onward we would go fossil hunting on holiday almost every year.

So, unlike many dinosaur paleontologists, I was not really inspired to study dinosaurs primarily. They were just one of many fossil species. Really, as a collector I would go out and look for any kind of fossils (except trilobites, which I am sorry to say I just don't find inspiring for some reason). I got into dinosaurs since they are very rare - you get to a point where you've collected lots of ammonites, clams, lobsters etc, and so you start seeking out vertebrates, since they're less common.

You are the Curator of the Dickinson museum center. Can you tell us more about the Badlands Dinosaur museum?

We were a small private museum opened in 1993 by Larry and Alice League to showcase their collection of fossils and minerals. In 2015, Larry and Alice retired and the City of Dickinson acquired the collection and hired me to look after it, and asked me to build the museum up into a "world class" museum. That's a big task, but we're working on it!

What dinosaurs do you have on exhibit?

For real dinosaur fossils, we have a good complete Triceratops prorsus skull ("Bill"), and a good postcranial skeleton which has an injured tail ("Larry"); the jaws of the Daspletosaurus wilsoni holotype skull; the articulated tail of "Denver's Tyranno" (the rest of the skeleton is being prepared in our public fossil prep lab); some eggshell; various teeth; a c.f. Brachylophosaurus arm with skin preserved; and a composite skeleton of an Edmontosaurus.
For exclusive casts we have the skull of a new species of nodosaurid (which I found in 2015). We also have three fabulous life-size feathered dinosaur models by Boban Filipovic, including his National Geogrpahic-Lanzendorf award winning Trierarchuncus, and an Acheroraptor attacking a Didelphodon.
In terms of non-exclusive cast or other skeletons we have a Stegosaurus and Allosaurus; a Gorgosaurus; Thescelosaurus; the LACM T.rex skull; a Stygimoloch and Stegoceras skull; juvenile Corythosaurus skull; a display of dinosaur claws, Saurornitholestes; a baby Triceratops; Archaeopteryx, Compsognathus, and three Pteranodon.

We also have lots of fossil mammals, fish, invertebrates, plants, and minerals on exhibit. We're currently working on new displays. It takes a few years for us to get our newest discoveries cleaned up, researched, and ready for display, but we have some really cool unique fossils on the way.

Do you allow the public to help with fossil digs?

Yes we take volunteers on our residential field work. Details on how to volunteer are on the museum website.

What Formation do you do digs at?

We work mostly in the Judith River Formation and the Hell Creek Formation.

Do you have a favorite dinosaur and why?

I usually say Baryonyx, since I collected various baryonychid teeth from the Isle of Wight many years ago.

Is there a species of dinosaur or prehistoric creature that you hope to one day find?

I will publish research on any dinosaur that we find. However, if there was one taxonomic group that I suppose I am specialised in, it would be chasmosaurines (horned dinosaurs). I'd really like to find a chasmosaurine from the bottom of the Dinosaur park Formation, or from near the top of the Dinosaur Park Formation!

Is there anything else you would like to tell us about the Badlands dinosaur museum?

We're open year round, so if you're in the North Dakota, stop by! We're also looking to open an online store that will be selling some exclusive merchandise based on our new research specimens and exhibits. Keep an eye on our websites!

Where can people go to find out more about the Museum?

The Badlands Dinosaur Museum's website:

http://dickinsonmuseumcenter.com/badlands_home/

And the best place is our Facebook page , which has regular updates with photos of new specimens, news from fieldwork, research, and videos:

https://www.facebook.com/dickinsonmuseumcenter

I have a twitter account that people can follow. It has similar content to the museum's Facebook page, but with some more personally written content.

https://twitter.com/df9465

Badlands
Dinosaur Museum
Open
Year-round:
Mon-Sat
9am-5pm
Summer:
(Memorial day
to Labor day)
Sun 12-5pm
Award-winning
new displays
DICKINSON MUSEUM CENTER
188 Museum Dr. East, Dickinson ND
dickinsonmuseumcenter.com (701) 456-6225

Meeting the men who re-introduced Daspletosaurus to the world

by Shetan Noir

image credit to Lindseywart

Shetan Noir bold black

Denver Fowler blue

Elias Warsaw red

Hello Gentlemen,

Can you please tell us more about your backgrounds?

I'm originally from near Manchester in the UK. I did my undergrad degree at Durham, then my masters at Bristol, then I did my PhD under Jack Horner at Museum of the Rockies in Bozeman Montana.

I'm currently an undergraduate student at Montana State University. I've been working with the Badlands Dinosaur Museum studying tyrannosaur evolution and behavior for the last year and a half.

How did you become interested in paleontology?

I have a collecting background. When I was about 5 or 6 years old my family went on a holiday to Weymouth, on the Jurassic Coast of the southern United Kingdom. When playing on the beach, I found the impression of a fairly large (~6") ammonite in a boulder and dragged it back to my parents (which took me about 20 minutes). My dad had an interest in fossils, so he took us fossil hunting to the beach Charmouth, nearby. From that point onward we would go fossil hunting on holiday almost every year.

I've been interested in paleontology for as long as I can remember. I remember watching documentaries about *Daspletosaurus* when I was 4 or 5 years old!

All photo credits to
Badlands Museum

You were both involved in naming a new species of Tyrannosaur, the Daspletosaurus wilsoni. Can you tell us about why you choose that name?

The name honors John Wilson, who found the holotype (name-bearing) specimen in 2017.

How best can you describe the appearance of Daspletosaurus wilsoni?

(I'll let Elias answer this one)

D. wilsoni was a large tyrannosaurid theropod (the group of dinosaurs including *T. rex*), with a skull measuring roughly three and a half feet long and a total body length of roughly 30 feet. Like other tyrannosaurids. *D. wilsoni* had a very powerfully built skull and neck, and would also have had the characteristic two-fingered hand of its closest relatives.

What sets the Daspletosaurus apart from other species of Tyrannosaurids?

(I'll let Elias answer this one)

Daspletosaurus was the largest tyrannosaurid of its time, although it was smaller than later members of the group like *T. rex*. It's most easily recognizable by the set of horns that surround the eye; *Daspletosaurus* had a large triangular horn just in front of the eye and a large rounded horn just behind the eye. These horns were larger in *Daspletosaurus* than any other tyrannosaurid.

With the set of eye horns I would imagine a dinosaur similar to Carnotaurus, Is Daspletosaurus a related species?

No, *Carnotaurus* belongs to a family called the Abelisauridae, a separate and more primitive group from the tyrannosaur family. Horns evolved independently in these two groups, as well as in several other groups of meat-eating dinosaurs (for example, *Allosaurus* and relatives).

Or is it a missing link in the Tyrannosaur family tree?

Some researchers don't like the term "missing link", but I actually think it works ok as the public understand what it means, and ultimately species like D. wilsoni are hypothesized as links between preceding and succeeding forms. I don't think the term implies anything about "progress".

Yes, we consider *D. wilsoni* to represent a "missing link" between the two other species of *Daspletosaurus*, *D. torosus* and *D. horneri*. This group has previously been suggested to be ancestral to *T. rex*, which is the subject of additional research that we hope to publish soon.

Can you explain the term anagenesis?

It's when a population of animals evolves over time without splitting into multiple lineages.

Anagenesis is the evolution of one species into another without branching. In the case of *D. wilsoni*, we are proposing anagenesis between the three species of *Daspletosaurus*, such that *D. torosus* evolved into *D. wilsoni*, which in turn evolved into *D. horneri*.

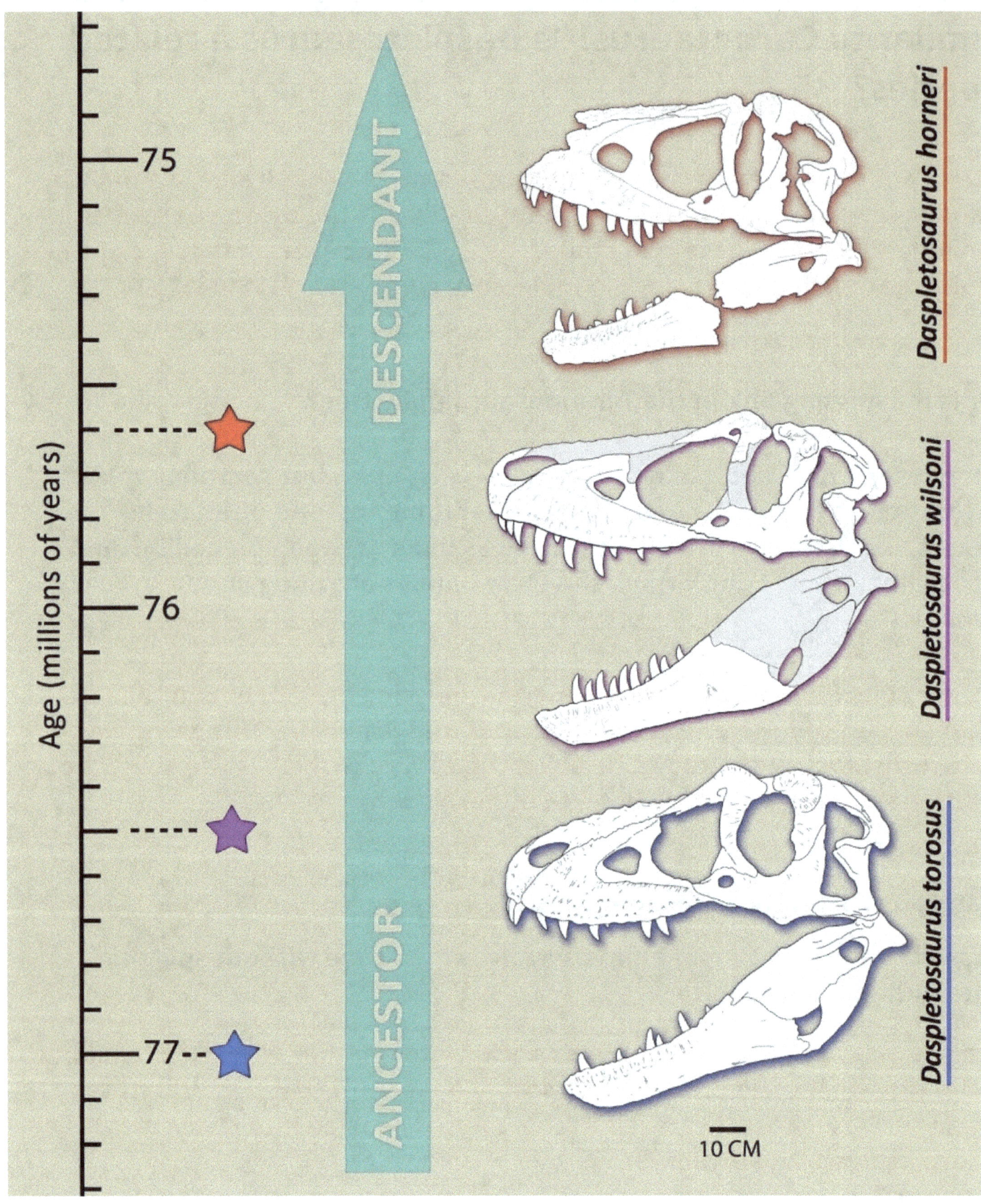

Age (millions of years)
75
76
77
DESCENDANT
ANCESTOR
Daspletosaurus horneri
Daspletosaurus wilsoni
Daspletosaurus torosus
10 CM

What was the diet of Daspletosaurus?

Based on the shape of the teeth, and evidence from related theropods, it was carnivorous. Direct evidence is less common, although in the same area as we recovered the D. wilsoni skeleton, we have found a number of hadrosaur bones with large toothmarks made by tyrannosaurs (likely, D. wilsoni).

Daspletosaurus was carnivorous, and probably fed on some of the large herbivorous dinosaurs that are found in rocks of the same age, like *Brachylophosaurus* and *Centrosaurus.*

Does the specimen you both research have a nickname?

The holotype specimen (BDM 107) is nicknamed "Sisyphus" after the Greek mythological character. The mythological Sisyphus angered the Greek gods, so was condemned to repeatedly move a rock up to the top of a mountain, only to see it roll down again. This gives rise to the term "sisyphean" describing an endless or hopeless task. When digging up the holotype we spent something like 6-8 weeks digging away rock overlying the bone layer.

We nicknamed the specimen "Sisyphus," after the figure from Greek mythology cursed to push a boulder uphill for eternity, as we had to move quite a bit of rock during the excavation.

Where is this specimen now, can the public see it on display?

The specimen is held at the public repository at Badlands Dinosaur Museum, Dickinson Museum Center, Dickinson, North Dakota, USA. We have the jaws on display currently, and are working on getting all the bones scanned so that we can make a full 3D reconstruction of the skull.

The jaws of the specimen are on public display at the Badlands Dinosaur Museum in Dickinson, North Dakota; the rest of the specimen is in collections and will be displayed once a full mount and reconstruction of the skull can be made.

What else would you like to tell us about Daspletosaurus?

Daspletosaurus has lots to tell us about the way that tyrannosaurs lived and evolved. Research in previous years has been hampered by the rarity of good specimens; while this will always be an issue across dinosaur science, Badlands Dinosaur Museum is continuing to excavate exciting new fossils that help to fill in some of the gaps in our knowledge. Keep an eye out for upcoming discoveries!

Where can people find out more about your research?

The Badlands Dinosaur Museum's website has details on our fieldwork and research programs:

http://dickinsonmuseumcenter.com/badlands_home/

The Badlands Dinosaur Museum has some web pages. Our Facebook page has regular updates with photos of new specimens, news from fieldwork, research, and videos:

https://www.facebook.com/dickinsonmuseumcenter

I have a twitter account that people can follow. It has similar content to the museum's Facebook page, but with some more personally written content.

https://twitter.com/df9465

I'll post any updates on twitter (@eliaswarshaw).

JOACHIM REGIONAL MUSEUM
Interview with
Dr. Elizabeth Freedman Fowler
and Dr. Denver Fowler
DICKINSON MUSEUM CENTER

"frightful lizard") is a genus of tyrannosaurid dinosaur that lived in Laramidia between about 77 and 74 million years ago, during the Late Cretaceous Period. The genus Daspletosaurus contains three species. Fossils of the earlier type species, D. torosus, have been found in Alberta, and fossils of a later second species, D. wilsoni, and third species, D. horneri, have been found only in Montana.

While very large by the standard of modern predators, Daspletosaurus was not the largest tyrannosaurid. Adults could reach a length of 8–9 meters (26–30 ft) from snout to tail,[5] and a body mass of 2–3 metric tons (2.2–3.3 short tons)

Charleston Fossil Adventures

By Shetan Noir

How did you become a paleontologist?

I received my degree from Appalachian State University. You can pursue a few different fields and still wind up within paleontology; biology, environmental science, evolutionary biology, and geology are all degrees that can lead to paleontology as a profession. My degree is in environmental science. Following graduation I worked at a state park in South Carolina as the interpretive ranger, and curated their fossil collection and museum for three years.

LEGAL   ETHICAL   SUCCESSFUL

Can you tell us more about your different fossil collecting tours?

We offer Fossil Adventures in increments of 2, 4, and 6 hours, geared towards beginner, intermediate, and advanced fossil collectors. These Adventures are listed on our website as the "1 Island Adventure, 2 Island Adventure, and 3 Island Adventure" where we visit, you guessed it -- 1, 2, and 3 islands, respectively. Our fourth offering is called the Prehistoric Plantation Cruise where we take clients past four of Charleston's historic plantations, and explain the link between post-Civil War prosperity in the south and paleontology. Charleston was once the world's largest producer of phosphate fertilizer, and this industry provided the cash injection our economy needed to rebuild from the destruction of the Civil War.

What can people expect on your tours, Can you tell us what a tour involves?

During the 1, 2, and 3 Island Adventures, clients are taken by boat to secluded shorelines that yield fossils dating back 30 million years. At the site, we simply scan the surface with our eyes to locate common and unusual fossils from the Ice Age and beyond. Believe it or not, incredible fossils wash out every day at these sites, with no sign of diminishing any time soon! We hunt the shorelines of dredge islands from the early 20th Century. During the historic dredging operations, machinery dug down into fossiliferous layers laden with shark teeth, whale bones, sea turtle fossils, and more. Now, thanks to currents from the rivers, prehistoric remains wash out with each retreating tide. During the tour we provide knee pads as well as collection aprons that our clients get to keep after their Adventure. At the end of our 2 and 3 Island Adventures, Ashby sits down with each client and sorts all of their fossils into categories according to the animal species and bone type. Following this sorting, our clients are invited to film Ashby as he narrates in great detail what the guests have found and what makes some specimens more unusual than others.

What types of fossils and teeth do you commonly find on your tours?

Fossils found in the South Carolina Lowcountry date back 30 million years. Our oldest deposits are marine layers containing fossils from toothed echolocating dolphins, leatherback and loggerhead sea turtles, a false-toothed bird with a 30-foot wingspan (*Pelagornis*) saltwater crocodiles, early sirenians (manatee & dugong relatives) sawfish, and of course lots and lots of sharks. Charleston offers a wonderful glimpse at our Oligocene oceans, and as such, one of the shark teeth we find most commonly on our tours is from*Carcharocles/Otodus angustidens*, aka megalodon's "grandfather", two species prior to the evolution of megalodon. Ice Age fossils we often find are teeth from bison, horses, armoring from giant armadillos, giant sloth teeth, semi-aquatic turtle shell, camel, and even rhinoceros remains!

What tips do you suggest for a successful fossil collecting trip?

First and foremost, a positive attitude! Coming in with unrealistic expectations is guaranteed to provide a let down when that 7" megalodon tooth didn't wash out. More practically, wearing closed-toe footwear, staying hydrated, and bringing your prescription glasses or readers to be able to spot smaller fossils or patterns are all key.

Do guests get to keep everything they find?

Absolutely! Unless we see any specimen that is scientifically significant and warrants donation, guests are allowed to keep all finds. Don't worry, this means you get to keep all of those shark teeth!

Are there any laws or rules about collecting fossils from the water or beaches? Do you need a permit?

Yes. The 1991 SC Antiquities Act protects all fossils and human artifacts older than 50 years that are found in our waterways. Any individual looking to hunt underwater is required to have a "Hobby Diving License" for the collection of these remains. This license should be called an artifact collection license, as it is required in any navigable waterway, regardless of if you are diving or not. Individuals with this license are not allowed to use tools of any kind, and must report their finds quarterly to the state. If, after 60 days, the state does not want anything collected, the individual is free to sell, keep, or otherwise distribute the artifacts they found. Beaches and shorelines do not fall under this law as fossils are *ex situ*, or, taken out of geologic context and of less scientific significance.

You also wrote a book about fossil collecting, Can you tell us more about it?

In 2020 my parents and I published *A Beachcomber's Guide to Fossils* through the University of Georgia Press. We worked for six years on completing the text, which has over 1200 full color images, 325+ fossils described, and a range applicable in the US from Texas east to Florida, and north to New Jersey. The temporal range is primarily from the Paleocene through the Pleistocene, although some older specimens are included. The book is presented in field guide format, sized 6x9 inches, and with 544 pages. Interspersed throughout the book are 12 "Species Highlights" where we cover the history of different animal lineages. We wrote the book in an approachable style, as a bridge between dry academic texts and the general public who genuinely want to learn more about our planet. To facilitate this approach, at the bottom of each identification page we've included fun facts and humour to lighten the more technical information above. Even if people only buy the book for the photos, they'll gain a greater understanding of what to look for when combing a beach.

Is there anything else you want to tell us about your fossil collecting tours?

CFA has operated legally and ethically within state regulations since its founding in 2016. We take great pride in our approach to educating the public, protecting the environment, and facilitating the donation of scientifically significant finds to local museums and institutions.

Do you have any social media sites or websites?

You can find us online at chsfossiladventures.com, on Facebook at "Charleston Fossil Adventures," and view videos from our trips on YouTube at "Charleston Fossil Adventures." We also have a Patreon account under the business name for the fossil identification services we provide.

CHARLESTON
FOSSIL ADVENTURES
SHARK TOOTH
CLUB
MON THLY

www.burpee.org/paleofest2023

March 3-5th 2023

PaleoFest
PRESENTED BY THE BURPEE MUSEUM

PaleoFest 2023 | Burpee